D1456791

Cover photograph by Jupiter Images. Photographs throughout the book are from: Comstock, Corbis, Getty Images, iStockphotos.com, Jupiter Images, Jupiter Unlimited, Photo.com, Shutterstock, and Stockbyte. Photographs on pages 44, 74, 84, 86 and 150, LDS Church Archives. Photograph on page 114, John Bytheway. Photograph on page 26–27, Lonna Tucker, Fripp Island Golf & Beach Resort, Ocean Creek Course–Hole no. 6. Photograph on pages 68–69, Lonna Tucker, Troon North Golf Club, Monument Course–Hole no. 15.

Visit us at DeseretBook.com

Library of Congress Cataloging-in-Publication Data

Bytheway, John, 1962–
  Golf : lessons I learned while looking for my ball / John Bytheway.
    p.   cm.
  Includes bibliographical references.
  ISBN 978-1-59038-909-6 (hardbound : alk. paper)
  1. Golfers—Religious life.   2. Golf—Religious aspects—Christianity.
3. Christian life—Mormon authors.   I. Title.
  BV4596.G64B98 2008
  248.4′893—dc22   2008006620

Printed in the United States of America
Publishers Printing, Salt Lake City, Utah

10   9   8   7   6   5   4   3   2   1

GOLF

Lessons I Learned While Looking for My Ball

JOHN BYTHEWAY

DESERET
BOOK

SALT LAKE CITY, UTAH

DEDICATION

To Michael R. Loveridge, my father-in-law, who, when I announced that I was going golfing one day said, "Can I come and just observe?" Shortly after, he decided to pick up the game himself. He is now one of my most frequent golfing partners along with my brothers-in-law Michael Dustin, Marshall Hendrickson, Jeff Loveridge, Christian Loveridge, Josh Mercer, and Tim Johnson to whom this book is also dedicated.

ACKNOWLEDGMENTS

I owe a round of golf to Chris Schoebinger, my product director for his encouragement, Richard Peterson for his wonderful editing skills and many contributions to this book, and to Richard Erickson and Scott Eggers for the beautiful design. Thanks always to Sheri Dew and Deseret Book for sticking with me over the years.

Golf is deceptively simple and
endlessly complicated; it satisfies the soul and
frustrates the intellect. It is at the same time
rewarding and maddening—and it is without a doubt
the greatest game mankind has ever invented.

ARNOLD PALMER

"FORE" WORD

IT'S TOO BAD we're not getting acquainted somewhere else, such as, say, the first tee. I'd extend my hand and say, "Hi, I'm John, it's good to meet you." (I probably wouldn't mention my last name because I've learned from past experience that the resulting explanation takes too long.)

After you saw my first tee shot, you might wonder what qualifies a guy like me to write a book on golf. Answer: I love the game. I *love* the game (except that one hole where you have to putt through a windmill). Kidding aside, a few years ago I bought my first set of clubs—woods, irons, a putter, and a bag for $100—and set out for the golf course.

In previous years I'd played a handful of times with borrowed clubs, but now I'd invested a whopping hundred bucks on clubs labeled "Made in China"—and I was ready to learn the game in earnest. What I didn't expect is that I would learn a lot more than just the game of golf.

When I first started playing golf, I decided that I would avoid renting a cart. If nothing else, I wanted the exercise benefit.

Walking the course, especially if you don't hit down the middle of the fairway, provides a pretty good workout AND gives you time to think. And there's no better place to think than in the outdoors, walking on the green

grass under a blue sky and enjoying the gentle breeze. Just another reason why I love the game.

By vocation, I am a teacher. Because of that, I am constantly thinking about teaching. In addition, I am always looking (perhaps too hard) for lessons of life, and I often find them while playing golf. Other golfers, golf instructors, and sports writers have also found life lessons in the game, and I've added some of their insights to my own. If you don't yet love golf, maybe these few pages will entice you to try the game, as well as give you something to think about.

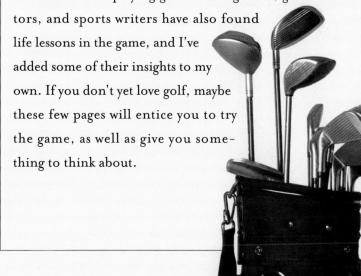

Golf is a good walk spoiled.

MARK TWAIN

THE GAME

> **Golf is twenty percent mechanics and technique. The other eighty percent is philosophy, humor, tragedy, romance, melodrama, companionship, camaraderie, cussedness, and conversation.**
>
> GRANTLAND RICE,
> *noted American sports writer and avid golfer until his death in 1954 at age 74*

G OLF WAS "so popular in the 15th century that the 14th parliament of King James II of Scotland decreed in 1457 that 'fute-ball and golfe be utterly cryed downe, and not to be used' because they interfered with the practice of archery, an essential element in the defense of the realm." Similar decrees followed in 1471 and 1491, but it appears that none of the three were effective.

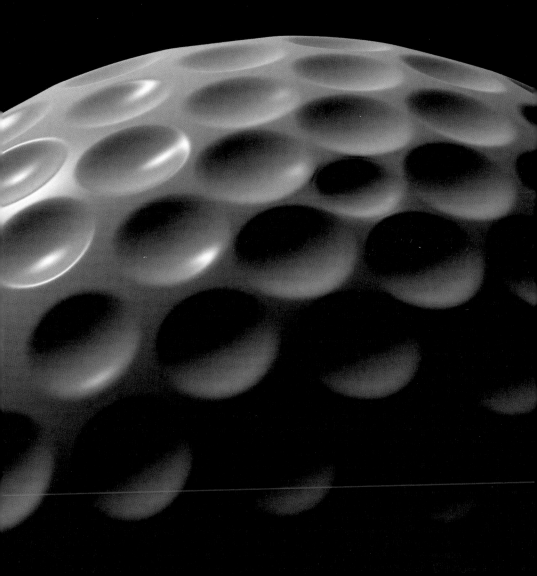

The only guy I'm playing in the last two rounds of the U.S. Open is myself.

TOM WATSON

JUST YOU
AND THE BALL

TEN-YEAR-OLD HARDY GREAVES: "It's the greatest game there is."

RANNULPH JUNUH: "You really think so?"

HARDY GREAVES: "Ask anybody. It's fun, it's hard, you stand out there on that green, green grass, and it's just you and the ball, and there ain't nobody to beat up on but yourself. Just like Mr. Noonan keeps hittin' himself with a golf club every time he gets angry? He's broken his toe three times on account of it. It's the only game I know you can call a penalty on yourself—if you're honest—which most people are. There just ain't no other game like it."

The Legend of Bagger Vance (movie version)

"THOSE WHO DON'T play golf have a hard time understanding the emotions the game generates. Everyone who plays, even casually, knows how crushingly disappointing it is to play poorly and how absolutely exhilarating it is to play well. But what must it be like to survive the enormous pressure of playing in one of professional golf's 'major' tournaments and actually win it? We saw a demonstration of how that affects a player in 1994, when Ben Crenshaw won the Master's Tournament the same week his beloved mentor Harvey Penick died, and Crenshaw collapsed in tears after holing out on the 18th green at Augusta, thinking how proud Mr. Penick would have been. Harvey Penick was a highly respected golf instructor, but his *Little Red Book: Lessons and Teachings from a Lifetime in Golf* contains as much advice on how to live life as it does information on how to play golf, and his students loved him."

RICHARD PETERSON

ONE OF THE things that appealed to me right away about the game of golf was that I could play it all alone. In addition, I had to take full responsibility for everything that happened. I could play one day and play the same course the next day and end up with a completely different outcome. Sure, they move the tee box occasionally, and they move the cup around on the green, but other than that, it's the same course. I've got no teammates, no coach, no fans, no home-court advantage, no road-game disadvantage, no one to blame but myself. And every day is a new chance to succeed, as well as another chance to fail.

I'VE DONE THAT

66 Golf is the world's most rewarding sport: In no other sport can an average player duplicate or even better a shot or score by the world's best players. Think about it. Can you dunk a basketball like Michael Jordan? Hit a home run like Alex Rodriguez? Score a touchdown like Jerome Bettis? Chances are the answers to all three questions is 'No.' In golf, however, you can make a par or birdie on the same hole as Tiger Woods; you can chip in from off the green like Phil Mickelson; and if you're lucky, you can even make a hole-in-one. Nobody in the world can do better than that. 99

HOMEPAGE *playgolfamerica.com*

MOST OF US AREN'T golf pros, we're not even accomplished amateurs. Most of us are "recreational golfers," which means we go when we can, not as much as we'd like, and we usually have time for only nine holes. When I first starting playing somewhat regularly, I was shooting in the fifties. Then, after a while, I broke into the forties, then the low forties. I'm a little embarrassed to admit it, but I started to chart my first year's golf scores on a spreadsheet. I even started saving scorecards when things went well. Every once in a while (on some courses) I'd break into the thirties. I won't soon forget when I birdied a par five (because I've done it only once). That felt good. What a game, when even an ordinary recreational golfer can make a great shot—a shot that a pro might appreciate, might even envy.

TO MULLIGAN, OR NOT TO MULLIGAN...

"Golf is a game in which you yell, 'Fore,' shoot six, and write down five."

PAUL HARVEY

"Golf is like Solitaire. When you cheat, you cheat only yourself."

TONY LEMA

"Take nine strokes off your score. Skip the last hole."

BOB HOPE

"I have a tip that can take five strokes off anyone's game: it's called an eraser."

ARNOLD PALMER

AS A NOVICE golfer with a desire to improve, I was faced with a tough question. Should I take mulligans? A mulligan is a free shot that says, "Let's just pretend that previous shot didn't happen." I was very tempted at first to allow myself one or two per game. But when you're throwing your bag in the trunk, you don't want to be thinking, *I wonder what I could've scored if I hadn't taken a mulligan?* Even worse, when you're telling someone about your score, your conscience tells you you'd better add a little footnote. I decided I don't want footnotes on my scorecards. I want a great score with no cheating, no mulligans, no do-overs. Also, if I return to a course I've played before, how can I measure my progress if I've used a bunch of mulligans? In life, I can't say, "Let's just pretend that didn't happen," although there are times I wish I could. Golf reminds me that I have to take full responsibility for my flubs and mistakes, all of them.

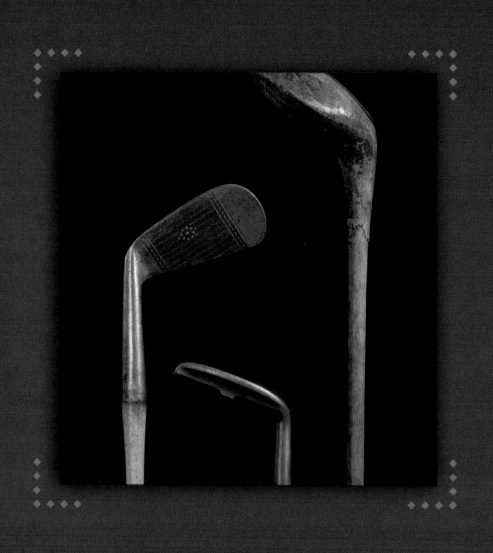

Listen to Your Bishop

Charles W. Nibley, the Presiding Bishop of the Church, persuaded the aging President Joseph F. Smith to take up the "ancient and royal Scottish game of golf" for exercise. President Smith did, and Bishop Nibley commented that the prophet was "excellent indeed for a man of his years." On one occasion, when President Smith was within about a hundred feet of the flag, he looked up during his stroke, topped the ball, and it rolled only a couple of feet.

He addressed the ball for the next stroke, began his swing, looked up too soon, and topped the ball again, moving it only a few more feet. He stepped up the third time and whacked it a hundred feet beyond the flag. His son, Wesley, called out, "Why, papa, what did you do that for?" "Well," President Smith straightened and said with a smile, "I was mad at it." Bishop Nibley said he laughed "hundreds of times" while recalling that incident.

❖ ❖ ❖

You may be wondering—after President Joseph F. Smith learned the game, did he entice any of his friends to also play golf? He sure did. You'll find the answer later in the book.

*The only thing a golfer needs
is more daylight.*

BEN HOGAN

The hardest thing to teach

an amateur is to

slow down their swing.

LEE TREVINO

THE SWING

> **"** Inside each and every one of us is one
> true, authentic swing. Somethin' we was born
> with, somethin' that's ours and ours alone.
> Somethin' that can't be taught to ya or learned,
> somethin' that got to be remembered.
> Over time, the world can rob us of that swing,
> it get buried inside us under all our would'uhs
> and could'uhs and should'uhs. Some folks
> even forget what their swing was like. **"**
>
> *The Legend of Bagger Vance* (movie version)

I BELIEVE THERE must be some sort of connection between beauty and truth. Have you ever watched someone with a beautiful golf swing? It stops you in your tracks. What is it about the swing that makes it so beautiful? It's hard to put your finger on, but you just know. It's similar to the feeling you get when you recognize that something is true. You just know. A beautiful golf swing is natural, fluid, relaxed—not labored or forced. Although you may not be able to perfectly describe it, you know one when you see one, and it often causes you to pause and say, "Wow—that was beautiful."

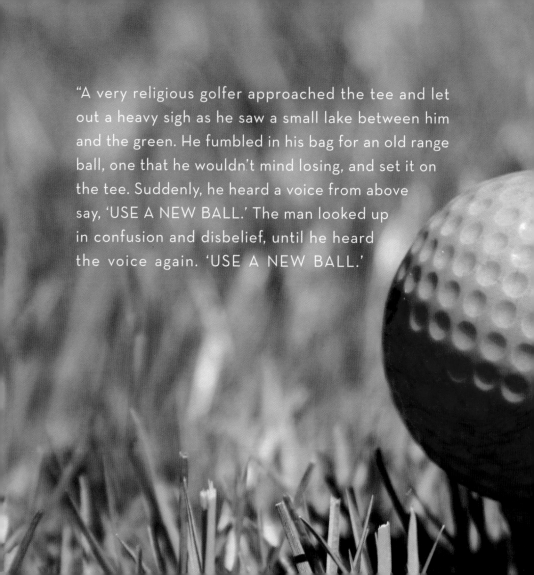

"A very religious golfer approached the tee and let out a heavy sigh as he saw a small lake between him and the green. He fumbled in his bag for an old range ball, one that he wouldn't mind losing, and set it on the tee. Suddenly, he heard a voice from above say, 'USE A NEW BALL.' The man looked up in confusion and disbelief, until he heard the voice again. 'USE A NEW BALL.'

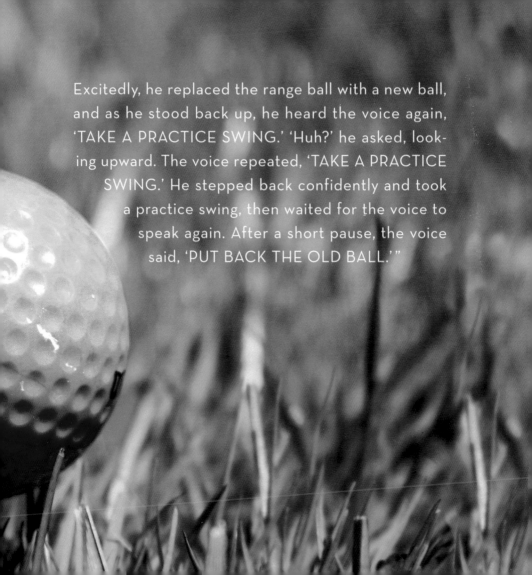

Excitedly, he replaced the range ball with a new ball, and as he stood back up, he heard the voice again, 'TAKE A PRACTICE SWING.' 'Huh?' he asked, looking upward. The voice repeated, 'TAKE A PRACTICE SWING.' He stepped back confidently and took a practice swing, then waited for the voice to speak again. After a short pause, the voice said, 'PUT BACK THE OLD BALL.'"

THE "SWING" THOUGHT

66 The golf swing has been endlessly analyzed,
and yet, it still remains a mystery, and only one
secret has emerged—one 'swing thought' that always
works, and that thought is, 'Don't think.'
But you can't just forget not to think. You must
remember *not* to remember to think. And you
must *not* remember that you forgot to remember.
It's a lot not to think about. But even if you
sometimes forget not to forget not to think
about your swing, there are ways to help your
opponent remember to think about his. 99

LESLIE NIELSEN

WHAT DO YOU think about when you swing? *Keep your head down, no outside in, don't be tense.* Personally, I try to clear my head. I used to think of all the things not to do, but now I try to be a little more positive. Maybe it helps, maybe not, but the advice of Corey Pavin rings true: "Instead of putting pressure on myself and thinking, *I've got to make this shot,* I just think, *Go ahead and make it.* It's a subtle difference but a big one." If focusing on the "dos" instead of the "don'ts" will take one stroke off my game—I'll do it.

THE SHOT THAT KEEPS YOU COMING BACK

66 Golf is one of the most dysfunctional relationships a person can ever have. Just when you're about to say, 'Forget it. I'm never doing this again,' the golf gods let you hole that chip shot, so then you say, 'Wait a minute. Maybe I'll stick around.' 99

SUSAN ANTON

HAVE YOU EVER had a really lousy game but finished the last hole with a beautiful drive? Most of my games are lousy, but the chance to improve keeps me coming back. "Well, at least I had a beautiful drive on no. 4," or "I sank a long putt on no. 8."

Chances are, you've had rotten days too at school or at work. You might even come home in a bad mood—then one of your children says or does something wonderful. And suddenly life ain't so bad, and you're ready to take it on again tomorrow.

GOLF IS
(OR CAN BE)
ADDICTIVE

After he was introduced to golf,
actor Jack Nicholson took an immediate
interest. Said he of the game,

" When you're bit—that's it. "

JACK NICHOLSON

"Heber, I Command You to Golf"

The addictive nature of golf is something President Heber J. Grant discovered. While serving as president of the Quorum of the Twelve Apostles, President Grant needed President Joseph F. Smith to sign some papers, but President Smith wasn't in his office. Feeling the business couldn't wait, President Grant hunted him down and found him on the golf course.

"Heber," began President Smith upon Heber's arrival, "you are tense and overworked. You should learn to play this game."

President Grant was stunned by the suggestion, feeling there was just too much work to be done.

"Many times," President Smith continued, "I, myself, get overworked, weary, and so tense I can accomplish but little. So I drop everything and come and play golf." He justified his pursuit by saying, "There is something about this game that relaxes me and causes me to forget my anxieties. When I get back to the office I can accomplish more in a few hours than I could in days when I am so tense."

Heber wasn't convinced. *"You will never catch me wasting my time playing that silly game. Now sign these papers and let me get back to work."* To which President Smith replied, *"No, Heber, I will not sign a thing until you take my partner's club and finish out this round with me."*

"Not on your life," Heber said. *"I've got too much to do to fool away my time here."* At that, President Smith spoke with authority, *"Heber, I command you to take that club and play out this round with me."*

"Well," Heber replied, *"if you're going to use your Priesthood on me I guess I'll have to."* President Grant endured a brief lesson and took his first swing. *"I swung at it,"* he later reported. *"I was very mad. I swung and knocked the ball a quarter mile down the fairway. Never since, in all my golf playing have I knocked a ball so far, and I have tried so hard and so many times to do it."*

◆ ◆ ◆

It was after that drive, we may suppose, that Heber J. Grant was hooked. Did he ever find the game frustrating? Yup, keep reading . . . you'll come to it.

RECOVERY

Three bad shots and one good shot still make par. Golf is a game of recovery.

WALTER HAGEN

Golf is not a game of great shots. It's a game of the most accurate misses. The people who win make the smallest mistakes.

GENE LITTLER

ONE OF THE WAYS in which golf so closely resembles life is that it is so hard to do perfectly. There are days when I'm all over the course. One time I hit my tee shot into an adjacent fairway—and still made par. In life, I'm all over the place, too. I judge wrongly, I serve awkwardly, my charity often faileth— I live far from perfect. Yet the Lord still invites me back to the sacrament table every week.

THE LONG GAME

> **❝** I'm hitting the woods just great,
> but I'm having a terrible
> time getting out of them. **❞**
>
> HARRY TOSCANO

EVERYBODY LOVES to go to the driving range and hit a bucket. One of the most soul-satisfying sounds in the world is the "tink" of a solid hit as the ball comes off the driver.

Some guys spend hours and hours on the driving range, and watching them strike the ball can be pretty intimidating. But there's one thing even more intimidating—the guy who spends his hours on the putting green.

Drive for show, putt for dough.

OLD GOLFING MAXIM

THE SHORT GAME

> **"** Low scores depend on how well
> a golfer plays once the ball is within
> 120 yards of the hole. **"**

BOB ROTELLA

> **"** Who cares if you drive it 250 yards
> if you can't get it up
> and down from twenty yards? **"**

ANNIKA SORENSTAM

THE LONG GAME is outward, observable. Step up to the ball and smack it. Without the short game, however, long drives aren't enough. The short game requires more thought, judgment, feel, finesse. To me there are parts of life that are long game: Go to Church, go to work and provide for the family, be where you're supposed to be. Other parts of life, the most important parts, are the short game—how I treat my wife and children, how I control and channel my thoughts, and my efforts to become more Christlike. The short game of life asks the most of me, but it also brings the greatest rewards.

Your biggest problem is that
you're standing too close
to the ball after you hit it.

BEN HOGAN

THE NEXT SHOT

66 All that matters in golf is the next shot. **99**

RALPH GULDAHL, *winner of two U.S. Open championships*

ONE OF MY favorite life lessons from the game of golf concerns the principle of focusing only on "the next shot." Don't think about the holes behind or the holes yet to be played. Just focus on what's right in front of you. Some people call it a cliché when a coach says, "We're not looking ahead, we're only thinking about our next opponent." But that's not a cliché, and it's not just "coachspeak." It's more like a true principle.

One time I had a great game going, and I knew it. But I started thinking way too much about what I needed to do on all the remaining holes, when I should have been spending all my mental energy and focus on only one thing—*the next shot*. I completely blew it on the last hole and ruined what could have been a record score.

There is no such thing as a golfer playing over his head. A hot streak is simply a glimpse of a golfer's true potential.

BOB ROTELLA

THE NEXT SHOT, PART II

> **66** Take therefore no thought for the morrow: for the morrow shall take thought for the things of itself. Sufficient unto the day is the evil thereof. **99**
>
> MATTHEW 6:34, KING JAMES VERSION

> **66** Therefore do not worry about tomorrow, for tomorrow will worry about itself. Each day has enough trouble of its own. **99**
>
> MATTHEW 6:34, NEW INTERNATIONAL VERSION

A MONTH OR so later, I was on the same course with another great game going. I focused as hard as I could on this thought: *What would I do if I absolutely had to hit this next shot straight?* That turned out to be the greatest game I ever played. I shot 33. (I'll let that sink in for a moment so that you can be impressed.) Par on that particular course was 31. Okay, now you're not as impressed, but two over par is a great game for me. No mulligans, no do-overs, no footnotes on my card, just a pure, honest 33. I didn't realize what I had shot until I left the ninth green and added it up. I was focused on the "next shot" mentality more than I had ever been, and I believe it made a difference.

Focusing on doing the best you can right now, *today*, without fretting over the past and worrying about the future, will eventually add up to a wonderful life.

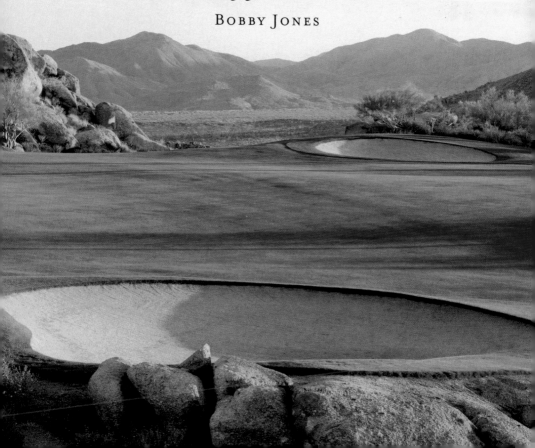

It is nothing new or original to say that golf is played one stroke at a time. But it took me many years to realize it.

BOBBY JONES

KEEP YOUR
HEAD DOWN

"Nobody ever looked up
and saw a good shot."

DON HEROLD

"The real reason your pro
tells you to keep your
head down is so you can't
see him laughing at you."

PHYLLIS DILLER

"There are two things you
can do with your head
down—play golf and pray."

LEE TREVINO

"You're looking up.
That's your problem."

*Graffiti on the underside of the roof
of cart 47 at Sea Scape Golf Course,
Kitty Hawk, North Carolina*

WHAT IS IT THAT makes golfers want to look up at the worst possible moment—the moment when the club is about to make contact with the ball? I've thought about it a lot, and I've decided it's a combination of excitement and impatience. We want to see the result of our swing as soon as possible—we want to know NOW what's going to happen.

However, in golf and in life, good things come to those who wait. Patience, as someone once said, is the ability to count down before you blast off.

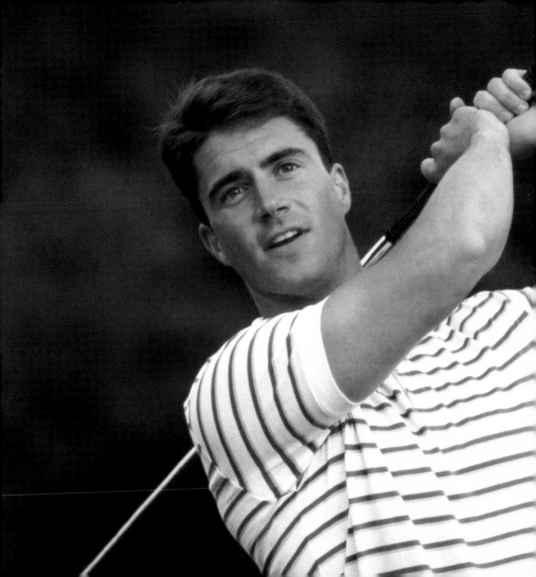

"I Never Swear, But . . ."

"President Grant took some lessons, felt he was in condition to play a round of golf, and invited some friends to be with him.

"On the first tee his friends insisted that he go first. He put the little white ball up on the little wooden tee and practiced a couple of swings. He was really going to show them what he could do. With a mighty swing he missed the ball. He stepped back again and took a couple more practice swings. This time he was really going to hit it.

"For the second time the club head missed the ball. This time President Grant was embarrassed and turned a little red. He stepped back for more practice swings. This time he was going to knock it a country mile, but the wind from the club head caused the ball to roll off the tee. He was frustrated. He turned to his friends and said, 'I never swear, but there are moments, and where I spit the grass will never grow again.'"

GOLFING
COMPANIONS

66 Golf is played by twenty million American men
whose wives think they are out having fun. 99

Jim Bishop

THE THINGS WE enjoy doing most, we enjoy doing with others. I don't know exactly what "male bonding" means, but I do know that men "bond" around an activity of some kind. You don't invite your male friends over to the house and say, "Hey, let's go in the front room, sit in a circle, and just visit." But you might watch a football game or take off for a round of golf.

In the past, when I've gone golfing alone, I suspected my wife thought I was being selfish. But when I started golfing with my father-in-law, my wife loved it. All I had to do was give her chocolate-covered strawberries when I returned. Fortunately for me, what she enjoys eating most, she enjoys eating with others (me).

PLAY YOUR GAME

66 On the first tee I looked at my caddie and said, 'I should hit a 3-wood here, but I'm with Arnold Palmer, and you don't do that with Arnold Palmer.' Then I thought, 'Hang on. I'm allowed to play my game.' I pulled out my 3-wood and knocked it right down the middle. The world was so much lighter for me now. I got back on my game plan, and I am very proud that I was able to do that while standing next to one of my heroes. 99

CHRIS HOY

ONE TIME I WAS invited to play golf with a former missionary companion and his friends at a country club. These guys were amazing players, and I felt completely intimidated and played horribly.

The experience was good for me, however, because it showed me how much I was comparing my game to others', rather than just doing my best. It also helped me to focus on par, instead of on my opponents.

Your Life Is Too Valuable Not to Play Golf . . .

" 'I wish you would play golf,' wrote President Heber J. Grant to Senator Reed Smoot. 'Your life is too precious and of too much value to the cause of Truth and our beloved country for you not to take care of your health.' "

◆ ◆ ◆

So did Senator Smoot ever play golf? The photographic evidence is on the next page.

LEFT TO RIGHT:

STEPHEN LOVE,

JAMES H. WATTIS,

PRESIDENT
HEBER J. GRANT,

PRESIDENT
C. W. NIBLEY,

AND

SENATOR
REED SMOOT

REPLACING DIVOTS

> **❝** If you want to take long walks, take long walks.
> If you want to hit things with sticks, hit things with
> sticks. But there's no excuse for combining
> the two and putting the results on TV. Golf is not
> so much a sport as an insult to lawns. **❞**

WHAT OTHER sport is there, in which the players of the game become caretakers of the playing area? Every player is expected to replace his own divots, fix his ball marks in the green, replace the flagstick, etc. Have you ever replaced the divots of others? I'll bet you have. If you've ever hit your tee shot into a divot, you know why.

I've probably produced more "divots" in life with my rash judgments and my big mouth than with my oversized irons, and I suspect I'll spend much of the rest of my life replacing those divots by saying, "I'm sorry."

A Gift for Generations of Golfers

On May 20, 1922, Presiding Bishop Charles W. Nibley donated to Salt Lake City a fifty-six-acre parcel of valuable land stretching south and west from Twenty-Seventh South and Seventh East, which today is known as Nibley Park Golf Course. "Born in Scotland, Nibley believed 'that this generation and the generations of men and women yet to come, shall find healthful enjoyment and rare pleasure here in playing that splendid outdoor Scotch game. . . . That thought,' he said, 'gives me the highest satisfaction and most genuine pleasure.'"

GOLF IS NO RESPECTER OF AGE

66 He enjoys that perfect peace, that peace beyond all understanding, which comes at its maximum only to the man who has given up golf. 99

P. G. WODEHOUSE

As a golfer ages,
66 The fairways get longer and the holes get smaller. 99

BOBBY LOCKE

A FRIEND OF MINE WHO is closer to 70 than 60 told me: "OVER THE PAST 15 years, most of the golf I have played has been the sort where when I got a little break in my work, I would run out to Glendale or Rose Park for 9 quick holes and get on as a single. That way, I could usually get right out—but almost always with strangers. With few exceptions, I've found the players to be congenial and pleasant. Often, the younger fellows would size me up, and I could see their initial reticence to have me tag along. 'Oh, no. This old guy's gonna be a drag.' But when they would find out I could play a little, there would be a marked change in their attitude, with them often asking me for some advice on what club to use or how to play a certain shot."

I N GOLF AND IN LIFE, you never know about someone else's abilities. One of the best lessons I learned while serving a mission among poor farmers in the Philippines was to live by the maxim: "Every man is my superior, in that I may learn from him."

PAR

> **"** Forget your opponents; always play against par. **"**

SAM SNEAD

> **"** If you compare yourself with others,
> you may become vain or bitter, for always there will
> be greater and lesser persons than yourself. **"**

MAX EHRMANN

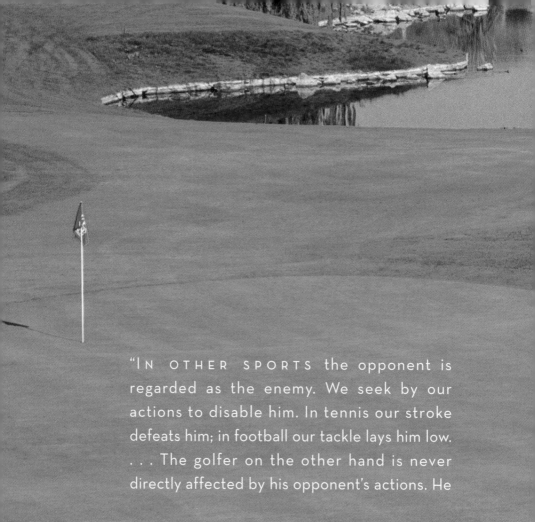

"IN OTHER SPORTS the opponent is regarded as the enemy. We seek by our actions to disable him. In tennis our stroke defeats him; in football our tackle lays him low. . . . The golfer on the other hand is never directly affected by his opponent's actions. He

comes to realize that the game is not against a foe, but against himself. His little self. That yammering fearful ever-resistant self that freezes, chokes, tops, nobbles, shanks, skulls, duffs, flubs. This is the self we must defeat."

BAGGER VANCE

SOMETIMES I ENJOY playing golf alone. People who have no problem calling me at all hours at home will apologize for bothering me if they catch me while golfing. My only competitor on those days is myself, and my measuring stick is par. Similarly, our lives will not be judged by how we stacked up against others; we all have different starting lines, different trials, different circumstances. We will be judged against ourselves, or as Joseph Smith put it, men and women will be judged "according to the use they make of the light which [God] gives them."

GOLF TIPS

> **❝** After taking the stance, it is too late to worry.
> The only thing to do then is to hit the ball. **❞**

BOBBY JONES

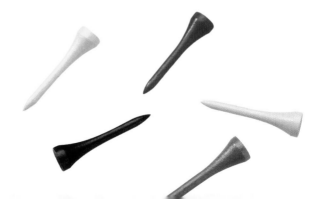

W HEN I FIRST took up golf, I subscribed to a couple of golf magazines. I must have memorized hundreds of golf tips. After a few months I had so many golf tips in my head, I nearly tipped over. I'd step up to the ball and try to remember a few of them, and there were so many I don't think it helped much. It's easy to get stuck in "analysis paralysis" and not be able to move forward.

Instead of trying to remember a hundred different things to do better, in golf and in everyday life, I do better if I focus on a few—the three or four things that will make the biggest difference.

"If You Hit Just One Really Good Drive . . ."

President Heber J. Grant felt that Elder James E. Talmage was working too hard and needed to take a break. President Grant frequently invited Elder Talmage to play golf. Elder Talmage refused, but President Grant persisted until they finally made a deal. "If you hit just one really good drive, nature will do the rest. . . . You won't be able to resist the game after that."

On the appointed day, President Grant, Elder Talmage, and other General Authorities gathered at Nibley Park Golf Course. After some brief instruction, Elder Talmage stepped up to the tee and smacked the ball 200 yards down the fairway.

"The spectators were momentarily struck dumb, then burst into enthusiastic applause.

"'Congratulations,' said President Grant, rushing forward,

beaming, with outstretched hand. 'That was a fine shot you will remember for the rest of your life.'

"'You mean that was a fully satisfactory golf shot?' [Elder Talmage] asked, cautiously.

"'It certainly was!' said President Grant.

"'Then I have fulfilled my part of the agreement?'

"'You have—and don't you feel the thrill of excitement? Now you'll be playing regularly. As a matter of fact, we can go into the clubhouse now and I will help you select a set of clubs.'

"'Thank you,' said [Elder Talmage], putting on his coat. 'If I have carried out my part of the agreement, then I shall call on you to live up to yours. You promised that if I hit a satisfactory drive and did not feel the spontaneous desire to play, you would stop urging me to do so. Now I should like to get back to the office, where I have a great deal of work waiting.'"

◆ ◆ ◆

I don't know about you, but if the President of the Church wanted to help me select a set of clubs—I'd let him.

RESPECT

66 A kid grows up a lot faster on the golf course;
golf teaches you how to behave. You start
playing with older people so that a kid who
plays golf is different from a lot of
athletes in other sports because he hasn't
had his own way. He hasn't been spoiled. 99

JACK NICKLAUS

GOLF TEACHES etiquette. Players respect other players. They don't talk while someone else is teeing off or putting, and they don't walk through—or even let their *shadow* fall on—the line of another player's putt. Playing partners, even opponents, tend the flag stick for each other or retrieve forgotten clubs for each other. And golf etiquette dictates that a player defers to a competitor whose ball is furthest from the hole. In professional and amateur tournaments, even the gallery is expected be quiet (unlike basketball, for example, where fans taunt, jeer, and scream when the visiting team approaches the free-throw line). The game of golf has assisted me in teaching my son to have respect for others.

FOR MY SIX-YEAR-OLD son Andrew's first game of golf, I bought a bag, four clubs (a driver, two irons, and a putter), and set out for the par-3 course. I rented an electric cart because I thought he might get tired of walking. It turned out he was rarely in the cart, but always *running* to his next shot. When we were walking off the 9th green, he looked up and said, "Dad, when can we do this again?"

HONOR AND INTEGRITY

> **❝** During the 1925 U. S. Open championship, amateur golfer Bobby Jones assessed a one-stroke penalty on himself because his ball moved as he addressed it. No one around him saw the ball move. Only he knew it had. When later praised for his sportsmanship, Jones bristled: 'There's only one way to play the game.' Jones lost the championship in a playoff the next day—he would go on to win dozens of others, later—but perhaps that was his greatest victory. No one had to ever question his integrity or his character as a competitor. **❞**
>
> DON WADE

"BOBBY JONES LOST the U. S. Open by one stroke. In calling a penalty on himself, he demonstrated for all of us the highest ideal of sportsmanship and personal honor. I'm prouder of him than if he'd won. There are things finer than winning championships."

"IN BASEBALL, a batter, knowing a pitch to be over the plate, will argue vociferously with an umpire to the opposite effect, trying to avoid having a strike called on him. The tennis player will bitterly contest a line call he knows to be fair, the footballer vehemently declare his innocence of a penalty he knows he committed. In other words they will lie. Deliberately. To gain selfish advantage. It is only in golf . . . that players routinely call penalties on themselves."

You Never Know Who's Watching You Play

A number of boys who grew up near the Nibley Park Golf Course enjoyed watching the men play. Sometimes they would wait by the ninth hole to see if any of the golfers would hit his ball over the fence. If a player overshot, the boys would retrieve the ball and return it to the player and would usually be rewarded with a nickel. The neighborhood boys were especially excited when President Heber J. Grant came to play.

"Unfortunately, at least for us," reported one of the boys in later years, "President Heber J. Grant tended to go straight down the fairway; he rarely hit any balls over the fence. But one time when he did, he gave a quarter to the lucky retriever!" This boy, who had his first conversation with a General Authority on one of those occasions, was Elder Neal A. Maxwell.

I MET THIS GUY
GOLFING . . .

> 66 I know I'm getting better at golf because
> I'm hitting fewer spectators. 99

GERALD R. FORD

THOUGH I OFTEN prefer to play alone, I've had some fascinating people join me on the tee. I've been in pickup games in basketball where, after a few minutes of play, you can have perfect strangers talking smack and trash. On the golf course, however, partners I've barely met give me "Atta-boys" and high-fives. One time I played with a young man who told me all about the Baha'i faith with the zeal of a missionary. I don't remember what I shot that day, but I have never forgotten the conversation. Another time, when I took my seven-year-old son with me to a par-3 course, a man with only one arm asked if he could join us. What an educational afternoon for me and my son. To watch a one-armed man scoring par! I've prayed for missionary opportunities, as we all have, and I've found more than one on the golf course.

Life ain't in holding a good hand,
but in playing a poor hand well.

OLD WEST EPITAPH

THE LIE

> **66** You know that in golf we play the ball as it lies. Now, we will not speak of this again, ever. **99**

BOBBY JONES'S *response to writer Al Laney who was distraught over Jones's affliction with a crippling disease in the late 1940s*

SOMETIMES YOUR ball lands on the groomed grass, sitting up beautifully for the next shot. Other times the only thing between your ball and the hole is a tree trunk. Sometimes it lands in a divot. That's golf, and that's life. You have to play the ball as it lies.

Golfer's 23rd Psalm:
May thy ball lie in
green pastures . . . and
not in the still waters.

UNKNOWN

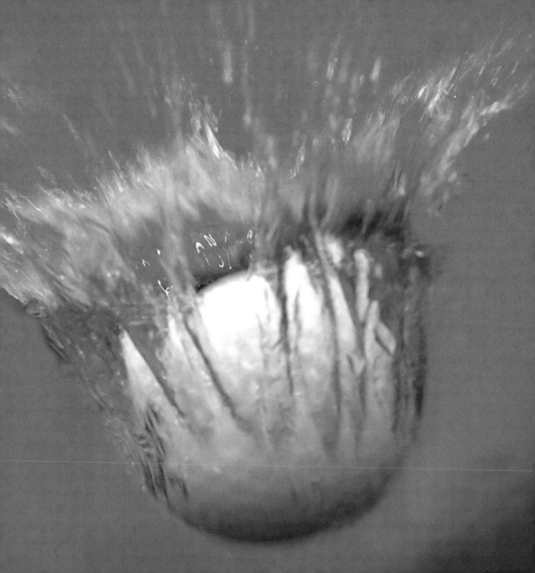

HONESTY

> **Golf is an honorable game played by an overwhelming majority of honorable people who don't need referees.**
>
> RICK WOODSON

> **Golfers should not fail to realize that it is a game of great traditions, of high ideals of sportsmanship, one in which a strict adherence to the rules is essential.**
>
> FRANCIS OUIMET, FEATURED IN *The Greatest Game Ever Played*

WE BELIEVE in being honest, true . . . except in certain sporting situations where we hope the ref didn't see. Just another way in which golf is a lot like life. The "no one will know" excuse doesn't work for those who believe in a higher power.

Grantland Rice, the noted American sports writer said, "When the One Great Scorer comes to write against your name, he marks—not that you won or lost—but how you played the game."

ADVERSITY

66 Golf is a five-mile walk, punctuated by disappointment. **99**

66 The secret is not hitting every shot perfect. The secret is getting the most out of the shots you don't hit perfect. **99**

BEN HOGAN

> 66 Golf puts a man's character on the anvil and his richest qualities—patience, poise, and restraint—to the flame. 99

BILLY CASPER

> Golf:
> 66 A game in which one endeavors to control a ball with implements ill adapted for the purpose. 99

WOODROW WILSON

Asked how he was playing, an aging Bob Hope quipped,

> 66 If this was a prize fight, they'd stop it. 99

BOB HOPE

"MOST PUTTS DON'T DROP. Most beef is tough. Most children grow up to be just people. Most successful marriages require a high degree of mutual toleration. Most jobs are more often dull than otherwise. Life is like an old-time rail journey—delays, sidetracks, smoke, dust, cinders, and jolts, interspersed only occasionally by beautiful vistas and thrilling bursts of speed. The trick is to thank the Lord for letting you have the ride."

JENKINS LLOYD JONES

FOCUS

66 In golf you have three or four minutes to think between shots. That gives you a lot of time to think about bad things. . . . Because you have more time to think in golf, it takes a stronger will to block out negative thoughts and be positive. 99

STAN SMITH

66 Once you've three-putted, you've three-putted. One thing about golf is you can't go back and erase your past. It's done. You might as well go to the next shot or the next green with a positive thought. 99

BEN HOGAN

THE GOSPEL ASKS us to think our thoughts according to a plan: "Look unto me in every thought; doubt not, fear not" (D&C 6:36). Yet we often dwell on a variety of worst-case scenarios of things that might happen to us. Joseph Smith taught that "doubt and faith do not exist in the same person at the same time" (*Lectures on Faith,* 6:12). Since you've got a choice, you might as well choose to fill your heart and mind with faith.

PUTTING

> **❝** Every shot counts. The three-foot putt is just as important as the 300-yard drive. **❞**
>
> HENRY COTTON

> **❝** Putting is always the great equalizer, because if you are putting well then it takes a lot of pressure off the rest of your game. You can afford to make a few mistakes if you're holing ten- and fifteen-footers for par. **❞**
>
> TOM WATSON

WHEN I THINK back to the best rounds I've ever played, I can describe what was going on in four words: "My putts were dropping." It's those little strokes that make a big difference. Similarly, life isn't about winning the lottery or becoming a star. It's about being a good husband, a good dad, and doing the little things every day to take care of your family. What's true in golf is true in everyday living: "Life isn't any big thing, it's a lot of little things."

HOWARD W. HUNTER

Did You Know?

One former LDS Church President worked
summers as a caddy at the Idaho Country
Club and once won the annual
caddies' golf tournament. Who
was it? Howard W. Hunter.
As a boy, Howard "earned thirty
cents for nine holes, and on a
full day Howard could caddy
for thirty-six holes, earning
$1.20. Sometimes he caddied for the golf pro,
from whom he picked up some good pointers."

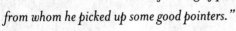

TARGET LINE

❝ If I hit it right, it's a slice. If I hit it left, it's a hook. If I hit it straight, it's a miracle. **❞**

UNKNOWN

❝ Forget the idea of a three-foot target area around the hole on long putts. Archers and pistol shooters aim for bulls-eyes, not the outer circles. Aim to make the putt. **❞**

TOM WATSON

I overheard a conversation between golfing great Arnold Palmer and a young caddie he was using for the first time. The young caddie, while handing Mr. Palmer his club, told him the distance to the flag was 165 yards, there was an unseen stream on the left, and a long and treacherous rough on the right. In a very kind but firm way, Mr. Palmer reminded the young man that the only information he required was the distance to the hole. He further suggested he didn't want to lose focus by worrying about what was on the right or left.

It is easy to lose sight of the really important objectives of life. There is much to distract us. Some are floundering in the water hazards on the left, and others are finding the long, treacherous rough on the right insurmountable. Safety and success come when focus is maintained on the important opportunities found by driving the ball straight down the middle—priesthood advancement, temple worthiness, and missionary service. And that's the way it is.

BISHOP H. DAVID BURTON

I USED TO JUST aim down the fairway somewhere, but now I try to be more specific. I love the occasions when I'm watching the ball in flight and saying to myself, "Wow. That went just where I was aiming!" Some of us practice the strategy of "Ready, Fire, Aim!" by acting without really knowing what we want or where exactly we want to be going. For example, some will spend more time planning their wedding than their marriage. If we have a target line in golf, which is a game, we certainly ought to have a target line in life, which has eternal consequences.

*The more I practice
the luckier I get.*
GARY PLAYER

PRACTICING

66 When practicing, use the club that
gives you the most trouble, and do not waste your
time knocking a ball about with the tool that
gives you the most satisfaction and with which
you rarely make a bad stroke. 99

HARRY VARDON

IF GIVEN THE choice, I'd much rather play a round than hit a bucket of balls at the range. (I usually don't have time for either one, so I'd rather play than practice!) It's interesting that in hitting a bucket I want to hit as many balls as I can (I always wish I had more when I'm down to the last few), but when playing a round, I want to hit the ball as few times as possible to get a low score. It's tempting to want to do what's fun to do, rather than do what's more difficult to do; but in life, doing what's hardest to do will help turn our weaknesses into strengths.

◆ ◆ ◆

"And if men come unto me I will show unto them their weakness. I give unto men weakness that they may be humble; and my grace is sufficient for all men that humble themselves before me; for if they humble themselves before me, and have faith in me, then will I make weak things become strong unto them" (Ether 12:27).

They call it golf because all of the other four-letter words were taken.

WALTER HAGEN

ENJOY THE GAME

> ❝ As far as golf, one of the things my dad kept instilling in me was the joy of the game. He made it fun for me. A lot of the times I see a lot of the kids, they don't enjoy being out there and that's a shame—you're supposed to enjoy the game; it's a game, ultimately. ❞

TIGER WOODS

> ❝ Keep your sense of humor. There's enough stress in the rest of your life not to let bad shots ruin a game you're supposed to enjoy. ❞

AMY ALCOTT

I F YOU CAN'T ENJOY golf, why play? One of the great contributions the Book of Mormon makes to our understanding of the purpose of earth life is as brief as it is profound: "Men are, that they might have joy" (2 Nephi 2:25). Sure, life is also about "misery and woe" (Moses 6:48), but don't miss the joy.

◆ ◆ ◆

"What other sport holds out hope of improvement to a man or a woman over fifty? True, the pros begin to falter at around forty, but it is their putting nerves that go, not their swings. For a duffer . . . the room for improvement is so vast that three lifetimes could be spent roaming the fairways carving away at it, convinced that perfection lies just over the next rise. And that hope, perhaps, is the kindest bliss of all that golf bestows upon its devotees."

JOHN UPDIKE

Life is to be enjoyed,
not just endured.

PRESIDENT GORDON B. HINCKLEY

Oops, Wrong Club . . .

Five months after being called to the First Presidency, President James E. Faust played a round of golf. He justified the practice by saying, "Playing nine holes of golf with Doug and Janna saved my life, and gave me a chance to breathe." President Faust's son-in-law observed that "it wasn't always easy for President Faust to leave the pressures of his office behind, relating, 'One day as we were walking onto the green to putt, I said, "Dad, are you going to putt with your seven iron?" He chuckled and said, "Oh, I was thinking about the budget appropriations committee meeting."'"

GENERATIONAL GOLF

> **66** My rule is that a youngster, no matter how small, should be required to hole every putt. If Junior grows up knowing he has to make all the short ones, that will automatically become part of his game. When he plays on higher levels and faces a two-footer to win an important match, he'll be ready. **99**
>
> HARVEY PENICK, *famed golf instructor*

I NEVER HAD THE chance to play golf with my father. He passed away just as I was becoming interested in the game. I have, however, played with my son. And that's a family tradition I hope to continue.

My friend Richard Peterson, who edited this book, shared this memory with me: "My dad and I used to play nine holes on or around his birthday in July. When he was 89, he had had a hip replacement and couldn't swing the club without pain, but we went anyway up to Mountain Dell where he rode in the cart while I played. We got out with two hot-shot players, young men, carrying their bags

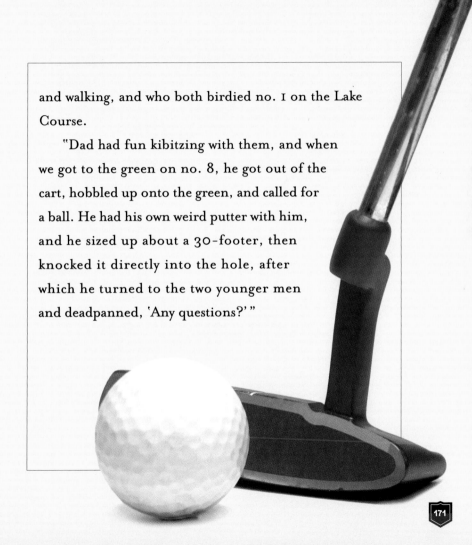

and walking, and who both birdied no. 1 on the Lake Course.

"Dad had fun kibitzing with them, and when we got to the green on no. 8, he got out of the cart, hobbled up onto the green, and called for a ball. He had his own weird putter with him, and he sized up about a 30-footer, then knocked it directly into the hole, after which he turned to the two younger men and deadpanned, 'Any questions?' "

"My doctor says I can't play golf."

"Oh, so he's played with you too, huh?"

GOLFING HUMOR

"A 'gimme' can best be defined as an agreement between two golfers, neither of whom can putt very well."

UNKNOWN

"Golf is wonderful exercise. You can stand on your feet for hours, watching somebody else putt."

WILL ROGERS

"The only time my prayers are never answered is on the golf course."

BILLY GRAHAM

"One under a tree, one under a bush, one under the water."

LEE TREVINO
describing how he was "one under" during a tournament

"Give me golf clubs, fresh air and a beautiful partner, and you can keep my golf clubs and the fresh air."

JACK BENNY

"I play in the 80s. If it's any hotter than that, I won't play."

JOE E. LOUIS

"If you think it's hard to meet new people, try picking up the wrong golf ball."

JACK LEMMON

"Columbus went around the world in 1492. That isn't a lot of strokes when you consider the course."

LEE TREVINO

His biggest game is over.

He putted out.

PASTOR EDWIN A. SCHROEDER
at Walter Hagen's funeral

*I've spent most of
my life golfing—
the rest I've just wasted.*

BUMPER STICKER

WILL THERE BE golf courses in the next life? Well, the scriptures do teach that "the course of the Lord is one eternal round" (1 Nephi 10:19).

GOLF IN PERSPECTIVE

> **❝** Don't play too much golf.
> Two rounds a day are plenty. **❞**

HARRY VARDON

IN PUTTING THIS little book together, I searched through hundreds of LDS books, talks, and articles to find any reference I could to golf. The vast majority of them were warnings against sacrificing the Sabbath day or church and family responsibilities for the game. Elder Neal A. Maxwell cautioned that we cannot "ride a golf cart into paradise." Noted LDS scholar Hugh Nibley, whose grandfather Charles W. Nibley donated the Nibley Park Golf Course to Salt Lake City, observed: "Like golf, [politics] is a game into which a man can put his whole soul without dedicating his life to it, which can engage his total concentration for a few hours a week, and then be put in proper perspective, even held in contempt, for the rest of the time."

Yes, it's only a game, and must be put in proper perspective. Our personal progress shouldn't be put on hold in order to shave a few more strokes off our handicaps. It's a game, but it's a great game, and I'll be playing it again.

So I'll see you on the range, or on the tee, or maybe I can round out your threesome sometime.

I have finished my course . . .

2 TIMOTHY 4:7

SOURCES

p. v. Arnold Palmer.
www.thinkexist.com.

p. 6. Mark Twain.
www.quotationspage.com.

p. 7. Grantland Rice. *The Quotable Golfer*.
New York: Main Street, 2004, 25.

p. 8. *Encyclopedia Britannica*, 1970, 551.

p. 10. Tom Watson. Charlie Jones and
Kim Doren. *Be the Ball: A Golf Instruction
Book for the Mind.* New York: MJF
Books, 2000, 192.

p. 17. Homepage,
www.playgolfamerica.com.

p. 21. Paul Harvey.
www.brainyquote.com.

p. 21. Tony Lema.
www.creativequotations.com.

p. 21. Bob Hope.
www.workinghumor.com.

p. 21. Arnold Palmer. www.ireland-fun-
facts.com/irish-golf-quotes.html.

p. 25. Joseph F. Smith anecdote. *Gospel
Doctrine: Sermons and Writings of President
Joseph F. Smith.* Salt Lake City: Deseret
Book Company, 1975, 520.

p. 27. Ben Hogan. *The Gigantic Book of Golf
Quotations.* New York: Skyhorse Pub-
lishing, 2007, 448.

p. 28. Lee Trevino. *Be the Ball,* 192.

p. 35. Leslie Nielsen. Leslie Nielsen's *Bad
Golf, My Way.* Videotape, 1994.

p. 39. Susan Anton. *Be the Ball,* 65.

p. 43. Jack Nicholson. *Golf Digest* maga-
zine. December 2007, 100.

pp. 45–46. Heber J. Grant anecdote.
Richard N. Holzapfel and William W.
Slaughter. *Prophets of the Latter Days.* Salt
Lake City: Deseret Book Company,
2003, 94, 96.

p. 47. Walter Hagen. In *Bobby Jones: Stroke
of Genius.* DVD. Directed by Rowdy
Herrington. Sony Pictures, 2004.

p. 47. Gene Littler. *Life Lessons from the
Game of Golf.* Colorado: Honor Books,
2003, 102.

p. 51. Harry Toscano.
www.midcoast.com/vquest/
Quote.hjtml.

p. 55. Bob Rotella. Quoted in Nick
Wright, ed. *The Best Golf Tips Ever.*
Chicago: Contemporary Books,
2003, 86.

p. 55. Annika Sorenstam. *Be the Ball,* 111.

p. 59. Ben Hogan. *Be the Ball,* 182.

p. 61. Ralph Guldahl. Robert McCord,
ed. *The Quotable Golfer,* dust jacket.

p. 64. Bob Rotella. *Golf Is Not a Game of Perfect.* New York: Simon & Schuster, 1995, 219.

p. 69. Bobby Jones. www.quoteland.com/asp?author_id=1126.

p. 71. Don Herold. Jim Apfelbaum, ed. *The Gigantic Book of Golf Quotations,* 268.

p. 71. Phyllis Diller. *The Gigantic Book of Golf Quotations,* 298.

p. 71. Lee Trevino. *Be the Ball,* 99.

p. 75. President Grant anecdote. Robert E. Wells. *Hope.* Salt Lake City: Deseret Book Company, 1994, 71.

p. 77. Jim Bishop. www.brainyquote.com/quotes/j/bishop105397.html.

p. 81. Chris Hoy. *Be the Ball,* 80.

p. 85. Reed Smoot anecdote. James R. Clark, comp. *Messages of the First Presidency of The Church of Jesus Christ of Latter-day Saints,* 6 vols. Salt Lake City: Bookcraft, 1965, 5:190.

p. 89. Anecdote on lawns. *National Lampoon,* 1979. www.golfun.net/joke115.htm.

p. 93. Charles W. Nibley anecdote. "Cooperation, Conflict, and Compromise: Women, Men, and the Environment in Salt Lake City, 1890–1930," *BYU Studies* 35, no. 1 (1995): 23.

p. 95. P. G. Wodehouse. *A Round of Golf Jokes.* U. S. A.: Exley Publications, 1992, n.p.

p. 95. Bobby Locke. *A Round of Golf Jokes,* n.p.

p. 99. Sam Snead. www.pasturegolf.com/trivia.htm.

p. 99. Max Ehrmann, "Desiderata." Cited in Thomas S. Monson. *Favorite Quotations from the Collection of Thomas S. Monson.* Salt Lake City: Deseret Book Company, 1985, 272–73.

p. 101. Steven Pressfield. *The Legend of Bagger Vance.* New York: Avon Books, 1995, 121.

p. 102. Joseph Smith. *Teachings of the Prophet Joseph Smith.* Sel. by Joseph Fielding Smith. Salt Lake City: Deseret Book Company, 1938, 303.

p. 105. Bobby Jones. Robert McCord, ed. *The Gigantic Book of Golf Quotations,* 130.

pp. 108–9. James E. Talmage anecdote. John R. Talmage. *The Talmage Story.* Salt Lake City: Bookcraft, 1972, 226–28.

p. 111. Jack Nicklaus. *The Quotable Golfer,* 48.

p. 117. Bobby Jones anecdote. Don Wade. *"And Then Jack Said to Arnie . . .": A Collection of the Greatest Golf Stories of All Time.* Chicago, Ill.: Contemporary Books, 1991, 86.

p. 118. O. B. Keeler, *Atlanta Journal* sportswriter. Cited in *Bobby Jones: Stroke of Genius*, Bobby Jones Film, LLC, 2003.

p. 119. *The Legend of Bagger Vance*, 121.

p. 121. Neal A. Maxwell anecdote. Bruce C. Hafen. *A Disciple's Life: The Biography of Neal A. Maxwell.* Salt Lake City: Deseret Book Company, 2002, 56; Neal A. Maxwell. *One More Strain of Praise.* Salt Lake City: Deseret Book Company, 98.

p. 123. Gerald R. Ford. *A Round of Golf Jokes,* n.p.

p. 127. Bobby Jones anecdote. *The Quotable Golfer*, 314.

p. 133. Rick Woodson. "Fifty Reasons Why Golf Is Better than Football or Baseball," *Rochester Business Journal,* 9 April 1998.

p. 133. Francis Ouimet. *The Greatest Game Ever Played* (film), 2005.

p. 134. Grantland Rice quotation. Grantland Rice. "Alumnus Football," in *Only the Brave and Other Poems.* New York: A.S. Barnes and Co., 1941, 144.

p. 137. Ben Hogan. *Be the Ball,* 182.

p. 138. Billy Casper. Jim Sheard and Scott Lehman. *The Master's Grip: Lessons for Winning in Life and in Golf.* Nashville, Tennessee: Countryman, 2006, 76.

p. 138. Woodrow Wilson. *A Round of Golf Jokes,* n.p.

p. 138. Bob Hope. *A Round of Golf Jokes,* n.p.

p. 140. Jenkins Lloyd Jones. In *Deseret News.* Salt Lake City, Utah, 12 June 1973, A4.

p. 143. Stan Smith. *Be the Ball,* 74.

p. 143. Ben Hogan. *Be the Ball,* 182.

p. 147. Henry Cotton. www.dailycelebrations.com/golf.gtm.

p. 147. Tom Watson. *The Quotable Golfer,* 160.

p. 151. Howard W. Hunter anecdote. Eleanor Knowles. *Howard W. Hunter.* Salt Lake City: Deseret Book Company, 1994, 43.

p. 153. Tom Watson. *The Quotable Golfer,* 160.

p. 154. H. David Burton. "And That's the Way It Is." *Ensign,* May 2003, 50.

p. 156. Gary Player. *The Quotable Golfer,* 74.

p. 157. Harry Vardon. *The Quotable Golfer,* 79.

p. 160. Walter Hagen. quotes4all.net/quotations/walter%20hagen/quotes.html.

p. 161. Tiger Woods. www.kive-quotes-and-quotations.com/golf-quotes.html.

p. 161. Amy Alcott. Thinkexist.com/quotes/amy_alcott.

p. 162. John Updike. *Golf Dreams: Writings on Golf* by John Updike. New York: Alfred A. Knopf, 1996, 149–50.

p. 165. Gordon B. Hinckley. "Stand True and Faithful," *Ensign,* May 1996, 94.